Moth

For Merlin, who gave me wings
—I. T.

For Elisabeth and Lars-Göran
—D.E.

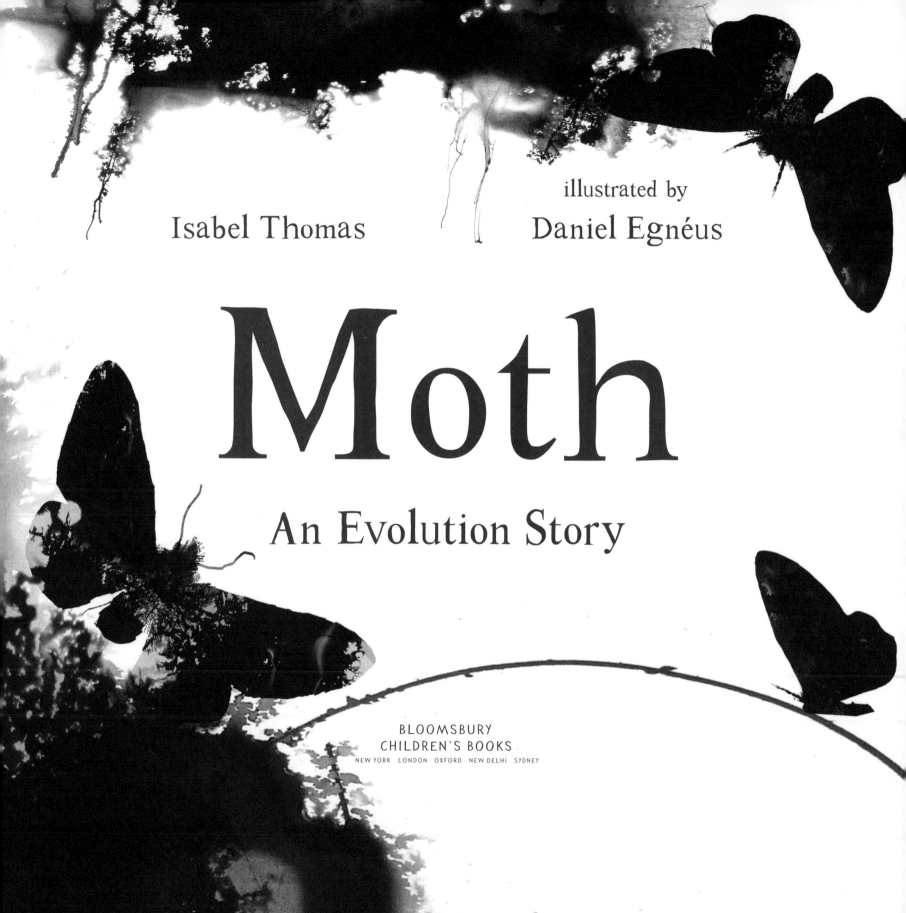

Isabel Thomas

illustrated by

Daniel Egnéus

Moth

An Evolution Story

BLOOMSBURY
CHILDREN'S BOOKS

NEW YORK LONDON OXFORD NEW DELHI SYDNEY

This is a story of light and dark.

Of change and adaptation,
of survival and hope.

It starts with a little moth.

PEPPERED MOTH
Biston betularia

A shiny cocoon wiggled
and jiggled in the moonlight.
Something was waking up
from a long winter's sleep.

Six little legs uncurled.
Two tiny antennae unfurled.
And four salt and pepper wings
stretched and quivered in the breeze.

But hungry predators were nearby.

Quickly, the moth flew away.

The peppered moth joined other peppered moths. Most had speckled, freckled wings.

But sometimes a peppered moth was born
with wings as dark as charcoal.

The moths flittered and fluttered . . .

. . . skittered and swooped . . .

. . . and looped the loop all night long.

They looked for food
and tried not to get
eaten themselves.

Oh no—a bat!

When the sun rose, the peppered moths
dozed on lichen-covered branches.

Silent, still, they hid.

Someone else was looking for food.
Who was the best hidden?
Who would survive?

Silent, still, the speckled
moths seemed to disappear.

But charcoal black wings were easy to
spot on the pale branches.

Dark-colored moths made
a feast for hungry chicks.

The speckled, freckled moths had the best
camouflage. Their salt and pepper wings
Kept them safe from hungry eyes.

They laid eggs of their own. The new moths
had salt and pepper wings too.

Every year, the same thing happened.

Hundreds of tiny eggs hatched.
The moths with the best camouflage
survived long enough to have offspring
and pass on their salt and pepper wings.

This is why most peppered moths
were speckled and freckled.

But then the world began to change.

People built factories and burned coal
to power magnificent machines.

They made steam trains
to take things here . . .

. . . there

. . . and everywhere.

Chimneys filled the air

with smoke and soot.

Pollution

stained the clouds
and blackened the branches
where peppered moths slept.

A bird went hunting for a snack.
Now the world was darker.
Which moths were disguised?
Which moths would survive?

Now the darkest moths had the best camouflage.
Their charcoal-colored wings kept them
safe from hungry eyes.

Now they lived long enough
to lay eggs of their own . . .

and their wing color passed on to

their offspring . . .

. . . and their offspring's
offspring.

Fifty years later there were just as many
peppered moths as ever. But most were
charcoal-colored. The speckled,
freckled moths were rare.

The moths adapted
to changes
in the world.

But that's not how the story ends.

Next time you scramble through
a forest or run around a backyard . . .

Be silent. Be still.

Look closely at the trees.
You might spot a moth with wings
as dark as charcoal. Or a moth
with speckled, freckled wings.
Because . . .

. . . people decided
to clean up the air.
They burned less
coal and found new
ways to power
machines.

Year

by year

by year

cities grew greener.
The air all around
became cleaner.
And the trees shed
their sooty bark.

Now the speckled, freckled
moths are camouflaged once more
and live long enough to pass on
their salt and pepper wings
to their offspring.

Today both colors of moth find
places to hide and survive.

They are still telling
their story . . .

. . . of light and dark,
of change and
adaptation,
of survival . . .

. . . and hope.

The Story of the
PEPPERED MOTH
Biston betularia

There are two variations of the peppered moth:

the light form

the dark form

An evolution story

The story of the peppered moth is a famous example of natural selection, the process behind evolution.

Until the early 1800s, most peppered moths were light with speckled wings. The dark form, spotted for the first time in 1848, was very rare. But fifty years later, the opposite was true. Most peppered moths had dark wings. The light form had almost disappeared.

Natural selection

In the 20th century, we realized that Charles Darwin and Alfred Russel Wallace's theory of natural selection could explain the transformation of the peppered moth.

During the day, peppered moths rest on tree trunks and branches. In the early 1800s, light, speckled wings provided excellent camouflage on lichen-covered bark. Dark moths were easier to spot, so they were more likely to get eaten by birds. Light moths were better suited to their environment, so they were more likely to survive and pass on their features to the next generation. This is natural selection.

During the Industrial Revolution, a huge increase in air pollution killed lichens and coated trees with a layer of soot. In this changed environment, dark peppered moths had the better camouflage. They became more likely to survive long enough to lay eggs, passing on their dark wings to their offspring. Over time, the proportion of dark moths increased.

Adaptation

Through natural selection, the population of peppered moths became better adapted to their new environment. The same process can also lead to evolution, where a group of plants or animals becomes so different from the original group that it becomes an entirely new species. Evolution explains how so many different living things came to be in the world, from tiny moths to modern humans.

The peppered moth was able to adapt quickly to the changes in its environment rather than dying out. This gives us hope that other living things will be able to adapt to changes caused by humans, including climate change.

The peppered moth continues to tell its story. In the mid 20th century, laws were made to reduce air pollution from smoke and soot. As lichens grew back and trees shed their sooty bark, the proportion of light moths rose again.

Today, you can spot both light and dark moths resting on trees.

The peppered moth is still evolving.

BLOOMSBURY CHILDREN'S BOOKS
Bloomsbury Publishing Inc., part of Bloomsbury Publishing Plc
1385 Broadway, New York, NY 10018

BLOOMSBURY, BLOOMSBURY CHILDREN'S BOOKS, and the Diana logo
are trademarks of Bloomsbury Publishing Plc

First published in Great Britain in 2018 by Bloomsbury Publishing Plc
Published in the United States of America in June 2019
by Bloomsbury Children's Books

Text copyright © 2018 by Isabel Thomas
Illustrations copyright © 2018 by Daniel Egnéus

Bloomsbury books may be purchased for business or promotional use. For information on bulk purchases please contact
Macmillan Corporate and Premium Sales Department at specialmarkets@macmillan.com

Library of Congress Cataloging-in-Publication Data
available upon request
ISBN 978-1-5476-0020-5 (hardcover)
ISBN 978-1-5476-0142-4 (e-book) • ISBN 978-1-5476-0024-3 (e-PDF)

Book design by Claire Jones
Art created with watercolor, crayons, acrylics, collage, and Photoshop
Typeset in Tom's New Roman and Times New Roman
Printed and bound in China by Leo Paper Products, Heshan, Guangdong
2 4 6 8 10 9 7 5 3 1

All papers used by Bloomsbury Publishing Plc are natural, recyclable products made from wood grown in well-managed forests.
The manufacturing processes conform to the environmental regulations of the country of origin.

To find out more about our authors and books visit www.bloomsbury.com and sign up for our newsletters.